Cricut for Beginne

The Beginners Guide to Master your Cricut M(
Projects, and much more.

Introduction

This book is about the Cricut Maker. It is the latest die- cutting machine from Cricut. If you have recently bought a Cricut Maker or are planning to buy one, this book is for you. Out of the entire Cricut range of machines, the Cricut Maker is the most advanced. It cuts and shapes more than 300 different kinds of materials. The Cricut Maker can be termed as the flagship machine of Cricut. It has been announced that any more blades or tips that will be introduced in the future by the company will be compatible with the Cricut Maker.

Cricut Maker is an extraordinary machine. It can cut, deboss, score, engrave, foil, perforate a large variety of materials. The best thing about it is that it can cut through lightweight materials like crepe paper to the much heavier materials like wood sheets and chipboard. This versatility sets it apart from all the other machines in the Cricut Family. The possibilities are unlimited.

The Cricut Maker is operated by a software known as the Design Space. All creativity and design are done through this program. This software is used for all the Cricut machines. It is an extremely user-friendly program. However, it might be a bit hard for a first time Cricut user. A detailed explanation of the usage is provided in the book. You can create your designs and start with some already installed projects that come free with Cricut Maker. You can also join Cricut Access, a subscription service from Cricut, where you can access hundreds of pre-made projects and fonts. You also have an option to upload and share your work with the Cricut community.

There are endless opportunities with your Cricut Maker. You can use it for your home projects such as cards, gift boxes, stencils, customized mugs, t-shirts, etc. You can also start your own business by selling your crafts and making customized merchandise for parties and events. You can also earn money by

giving tutorials of your DIY Cricut crafts. It is a horizon of possibilities.

Chapter 1. The Cricut Maker

(The Cricut Maker)

The Cricut Maker is the most evolved of the Cricut family. It is the most powerful machine till now. With the Cricut Maker, you have so many possibilities at your fingertips. It will take your creative potential to a whole new level. The functions are not limited to cutting only. It can engrave, emboss, score, and foil as well. All these functions are explained in the following chapters. First, we will start with the exceptional qualities and features of this extraordinary machine:

- It can cut and shape up to 300+ different materials. This capability sets it ahead of every other machine available.
- The project size it can create usually is 12inches by 12inches. The maximum size it can create is 12inches by 24inches in length.
- The Cricut Maker is perfect for professional-level DIY projects because of its ability to cut various materials, precision, and accuracy.
- The Design Space software it uses is compatible with iOS, Mac, Android, and Windows.

- It can be connected to the computer or other device with a USB port as well as Bluetooth.
- It can be effectively used for small businesses due to its commercial-grade performance.
- It has more than ten blades and tips for various functions.

- The Cricut Maker cuts with a pressure of 4kg. It is ten times more than any other machine. Not only does it cut with this pressure, but it has a built-in sensor to guide it to cut with adequate pressure according to the material with brilliant precision.
- The Cricut Maker has a new feature of the adaptive tool system. This means that it is compatible and will fit with all the available Cricut tools. It will be compatible with all the new tools to be released by Cricut in the future. Thus the need for upgrading your Cricut machine will not be required.
- The Cricut Maker has a unique rotary tool that is used for cutting all kinds of fabric. This is a new blade and is exclusive to the Cricut Maker.
- If you are working with a smartphone or a tablet, the Cricut Maker has a docking slot for them to be placed. This helps a lot while designing the projects.
- With the Cricut Machine purchase, you get access to fifty pre-programmed projects, including twenty-five sewing projects.
- With the purchase of a Cricut Maker, you get a free trial period for Cricut Access.

With all these features, your imagination can become a reality with just a little effort. For the first time buyer of the Cricut Maker, the blades and equipment can be intimidating. The thought of understanding and running a whole new software can also be a scare for some. But do not you worry. We have all of that covered.

In our following chapter, we will discuss all the Cricut Maker hardware and features, and in the next chapter, we will explain the Design Space software in depth.

Unboxing of the Cricut Maker

We have entered the most exciting part of our book. The unboxing of the Cricut Maker. Currently, the Cricut Maker is available in five different colors:

1. Lilac
2. Blue
3. Rose
4. Mint
5. Champagne

The Cricut Maker is sold stand-alone and with an Essential bundle option and the Everything Bundle option. The Essential Bundle includes some stuff to start a new project. These might be Cricut types of vinyl, Cricut textured paper, and Cricut cardstock. Similarly, the Everything Bundle also includes helpful materials to start away new projects immediately. Here we will discuss all the standard Cricut Maker and what comes with a basic Cricut Maker. When you open your Cricut Maker, you will find the following stuff:

- Cricut Maker machine
- Instruction Booklet
- One black fine tip pen
- 50 free projects in Design Space for practice
- Materials for a practice project
- Power adapter
- USB cable
- Light Grip Machine Mat (Standard Size)
- Pink Colored Fabric Grip Mat (Standard Size)
- Rotary Blade with housing
- Fine point blade with housing
- Trial membership for Design Access (Free)

Sometimes the fine point blade with the housing is already installed in the Cricut Maker. So, do not worry if you cannot find it right away. First, check inside the Cricut Maker. Most probably, the blade is already installed.

Cricut Blades

As mentioned earlier, the Cricut maker can cut more than 300 materials. But since each material has different characteristics, so the blades for their cutting are also different. The Cricut Maker is the most advanced in the Cricut Machines. It has the greatest number of blades compatible with its hardware. The best thing about the Cricut Maker is that in the future, when Cricut makes any more blades, they are all going to be compatible with the Cricut Maker. So, to invest in the Cricut maker should prove to be a sagacious decision. This chapter will discuss all the blades compatible with the Cricut Maker, their specific housing, and their usage.

(Cricut Blades and Tips)

- Fine Point Blade

The housing for this blade is either golden or silver. The fine point blade is used to cut light to medium weight materials. Some materials that can be cut using the fine point blade are:

- Crepe paper
- Simple paper
- Textured paper
- Cardstock
- Iron on viny

If you are a beginner, this blade is just for you.

- Deep Cut Blade

This blade has black housing. This blade cuts deeper than the fine point blade. The materials that can be used to cut with this blade are medium-weight materials. Following materials are advised to be cut using the deep cut blade:

- Thick cardstock
- Magnetic strips

- Chipboard
- Foam sheets
- Soft leather

This is also a handy blade for slightly more detailed projects.

- Bonded Fabric Blade

This blade has a pink housing. As the name specifies, this blade is a fabric only band. This can be used to cut:

- Bonded fabrics
- Fabric with and iron on the backs

This blade is compatible with the Cricut Explorer machine as well.

Blades Exclusive to the Cricut Maker

The Cricut Maker is the most advanced of the Cricut familu and it has the most number of blades and cutting tools. Along with cutting the Cricut Maker has a number of speciality blades and tips for functions other than cutting. It has more than eleven functional blades and tips. Also, the best thing is that Cricut has announced that if it launches any more speciality tools or blades, the will be compatible with the cricut maker. So if you have a cricut maker, you do not need to worry about changing your machine any time soon.

Here is a detailed explanation of all the blades and speciality tips of the cricut maker:

- Rotary Blade

Now, this blade is a significant feature of the Cricut Maker. This rotary blade is exclusive to the Cricut Maker. This blade has a silver housing. The specialty of this blade is that it will cut through any fabric. Apart from the fabric, it can cut cork and tissue paper.

- Knife Blade

This blade is exclusive to the Cricut Maker. It is not a part of the blades provided with the Cricut Maker. S, you must buy this separately. This blade is used to cut through much thicker material. Such as:

- Thick leather
- Chipboard
- Think wood
- Magnetic strip

This feature can be helpful with a lot of materials that cannot be cut with regular scissors.

Specialty tools For Cricut Maker

Apart from all the blades, there are some special tools for other functions other than only cutting.

- Pens and Markers

With the slots for the blade housings, there is a slot for pens and markers. This is used if you want to make greeting cards and want beautiful fonts. There is a variety of pens and markers compatible with the Cricut. You must buy Markers and Pens separately.

- Quick Swap Housing and Tips

This is a single housing, and several function tips can be used with the same housing. Following is an explanation regarding the tips that can be used interchangeably with this housing.

- Scoring Wheel

This is a unique feature. If you do not need to cut in a design but fold a piece of material, this scoring wheel is your friend. The uses for this feature are:

  - Making custom boxes
  - Making greeting cards

There are two types of scoring tips, single and double. You can use the same housing for both types of tips, depending on your project.

- Foil Transfer Tip

This one is one of the latest features of the Cricut Maker. This is used to decorate and add bling to the creations. It is used with foil sheets.

- Engrave tip

This tip can be used to engrave different materials with either texts or monograms. It works better on sturdy materials such as plastic sheets, metal sheets, and leather. You can personalize your designs with this tip.

- Deboss tip

This one is like the engraving tip but is more specific for softer and lighter materials. It can be used to decorate foil, thick card stock, and basswood.

- Perforation Tip

Sometimes a project requires tear-off materials. for this purpose, the perforation tip is used. This tip is more compatible with lightweight materials

- Wavy tip

This tip is handy for making greeting cards. This gives wavy edges, which give a decorative finish. It can be used to design the edges of cards, can be used for iron-on vinyl and other textured papers.

Cricut Grip Mats

(Cricut Grip Mats)

Cricut maker comes with Grip Machine mats. When you buy a Cricut Maker, it comes with one Standard Fabric Grip Machine Mat and the other Standard Light Grip Machine Mat. So, what exactly are the grip mats? Mats provide the surface for the material to be cut. The choice of mats depends upon the material you are working with. There is a different mat for different materials. Cricut has four different types of mats.

- Fabric Grip Machine Mat
- Light Grip Machine Mat
- Standard Grip Machine Mat
- Strong Grip Machine Mat

Each mat has a different color. All the mats have a protective cover of a transparent sheet to save the mat from dirt and dust. The out rim of all the mats is smooth, and the whole of the inner part has a sticky surface. The sticky surface is for the easy adherence of the cutting materials to the mat. The stickiness depends on the materials being cut. All the mats are calibrated into 1-inch squares. The centimeter measurements are also given at the bottom and right sides of the mats. Each of these mats is available in two sizes. The standard size is 12 by 12 inches, and the larger one is 12 by 24 inches for bigger projects. The importance of the mats lies in the fact that you will require these mats for all the projects. All materials require a surface to be placed and loaded into the machine. The mats provide this surface. Here is a detailed explanation of the functionality of each mat.

Fabric Grip Machine Mat:

(Cricut Fabric Grip Mat)

As the name suggests, this mat is for fabrics. The fabric mats are pink in color. It has adequate stickiness for all types of fabrics. When you use the rotary blade for the cutting of fabric, this mat is required. The mat catches dust quite easily, so it needs a lot of care.

Light Grip Machine mat:

(Cricut Light Grip Mat)

This mat is blue. This has the least amount of stickiness. So, this one is used for lightweight materials. The materials suitable for this mat are:

- Simple paper
- Regular vinyl
- Thin cardstock
- Crape Paper

Standard Grip Machine Mat:

(Cricut Standard Grip Mat)

This mat is green in color. This mat can be used for almost all the materials you might want to cut. You might use this mat for most of your projects. It can adhere to materials more than the light grip mat. The materials that can be cut with it are:

- Simple cardstock
- Removable vinyl
- Heat transfer vinyl
- Permanent vinyl
- Infusible ink transfer sheets
- Textured paper
- Embossed cardstock

Strong Grip Machine Mat:

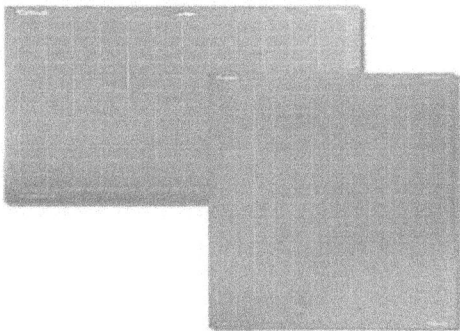

(Cricut Strong Grip Mat)

This is the purple color mat. This is meant for heavy-duty materials. Examples of such materials are:

- Balsa and Basswood
- Chipboard
- Magnetic sheets
- Leather
- Glitter cardstock
- Wood sheets
- Thick cardstock

Care and Longevity of the Mat:

The mats are expensive, so you might be interested in keeping them in use for a long while. The only way to increase a mat's life is to use it carefully and take good care of it. Here are a few pointers regarding the care procedure for these mats:

- Always replace the transparent cover/film on the mat after usage. This will protect the mat from unnecessary dirt and dust.

- After every use, a lint roller over the mat surface to get rid of any material residue.
- Clean the mat with non-alcoholic wipes.
- Except for the fabric mat, wash your mats with soapy water. The fabric mat is different from all the other mats and cannot be cleaned with water.
- Except for the fabric mat, use a scraper to remove all material residue to clear the mat surface.

Chapter 2. Design Space Software

The most significant aspect of designing projects is construction space. The basic program in which all the templates and layouts for cutting is produced is Design Space. You need to go to the Cricut website first and then download the Design Space software. For both your desktop and other Android and iOS devices, this service is made available. After download, you must sign up with the Cricut and build a personalized account. Now, you are set for your first creation.

For some, knowing about a new application may be an overwhelming activity. The Design Space, however, is a consumer-friendly program. The interface is simple and straightforward. However, before beginning any project, it is often best to understand Dthe applications. The program will be needed for all projects on the Cricut Makar. so, before getting into a project, it is necessary to have previous knowledge about the software. Design Space is described, step-by-step with illustrations in the following chapter to make it easier for you to comprehend.

The Design Space Home Page

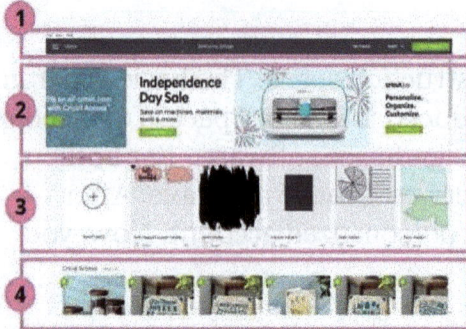

(Homepage Layout)

The first page is the Design Space as you open the app. The homepage has four parts. The topmost being the header, then the banner, which has all the Cricut promotions and offers. The other two sections are my designs and the featured material.

Four Sections of Homepage

Here is a detailed description of the Design Space Homepage. All four parts will be explained in depth.

- The Header
- The Banner
- My Projects Section
- Featured Projects

The Header

On the left side is the menu icon. This has two options, the homepage, and the canvas. This icon helps you to switch from homepage to canvas and then back. Apart from switching between the homepage and canvas, this menu also has other function options.

- New Machine Setup
- Print then Cut Calibration
- Manage Custom Materials
- Update filmware
- Account details
- Link Cartridges
- Cricut Access
- Settings
- Legal
- New Features
- Country Selection
- Help

As Design Space is the software used for all the other Cricut machines, you need to set up your new machine from here. Any calibration required is adjusted with the cut, then print calibration. You can manage your account settings. The Cricut Access icon is for the subscription. The settings icon is for your canvas setting selection. You can select your country, and there is a Help icon with a lot of frequently asked questions and their answers.

The Banner

This space is for Cricut advertisements and promotions. Any news about new accessories, ongoing promotions, deals, and offers are advertised here.

My Projects

This place will be blank when you first start. When you make and save a project, it will be stored in this area. All your projects will be profiled in this area in order of recent to oldest. This will make it easy for you to scan all your projects and repeat another project if you want to.

Featured Projects

This area will show you all the projects that Cricut provides you which are ready to make. In these files, you must select a file and click make it, and the rest will be guided to you. All the materials, design, blades, and the order in which the materials must be cut, all will be guided to you through Design Space.

The Canvas Layout

To get to the canvas from the home page. There are three locations where you can get to the canvas. the picture has highlighted all those three locations:

(How to reach the canvas)

The Canvas Layout

(Canvas Lyout)

When you open the Canvas, this is divided into four major parts. In this chapter, we will discuss all these four parts in detail. We will walk you through each part separately, and hopefully, you will be at east towards the end of the chapter. Once you understand all these parts, you will be ready for your first project. The canvas screen is divided into the following parts:

- The Header and Edit Panel
- The Insert Menu for Project
- The Menu for Layers
- The Creative Field or Main Canvas

Header and Edit Panel

Design Space Canvas page's top region is essentially divided into two sections.

Header

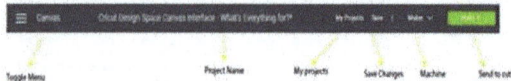

(The Header)

In the extreme right of the header is the toggle menu. In the center, the name of the project will appear. If you have not saved the project, Untitled Project appears at the center of the header. On the right side are the system selection and the 'Make It' button.

Toggle Menu

Click this icon, and you will find a new options dropdown. This is the same menu you find on the homepage.

Project Name

In the center of the header will be displayed the project name. Until you name your project, Untitled project is written in this space. You can name a project only after you have inserted one image or text into the canvas space.

Type of Machine

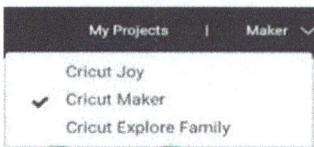

(Cricut Machine Selection)

As the Design Space is used for all the Cricut Machines, it is essential to select Cricut Maker from this dropdown. As some functions are exclusive to the Cricut Maker, if you have not selected the Cricut Maker, you will not see those functions displayed in the design space.

Make It

When you are done designing, save your files and upload them. Next, click on Make It. After this, you will have to select the correct blades and materials for cutting. All the guidelines will be given to you by design space regarding what to place on the mats and which material must be cut first if you are working with more than one material.

Below the header is the Edit Panel. It is to edit and organize components. You can select what sort of font might be suitable for the project using this panel. This is a taskbar where a lot of options are present. You might get a bit overwhelmed, but the functions and icons are straightforward to use once you get the hang of it.

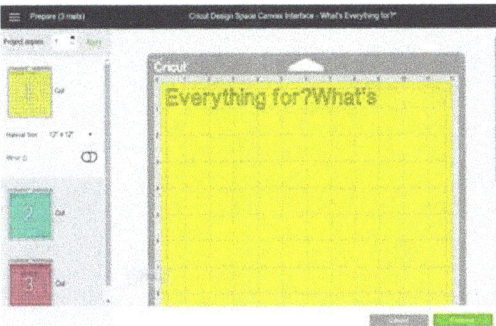

(Prepare Screen for Project Layers)

The Edit Panel

The resizing, text addition, alignment of projects, addition, and deletion of shapes and fonts, redo, and undo, all on the canvas, can be controlled at this Edit panel. A full description of each part is explained in the whole chapter.

(Edit Toolbar)

1.Redo, Undo Icon

We often make errors when working. These icons are a perfect way to fix mistakes. When an error is made, press Undo. Whenever you unintentionally remove something , press the Redo icon to get it back.

2.Fill, Linetype Icon

This choice would inform your device what equipment and the blades you would be using. you have options depending on the machine you have, in this case, The Cricut Maker.

Linetype

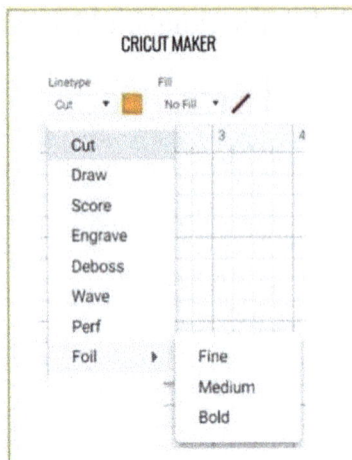

(Linetype and Fill Icon)

Here you will choose the type of blade you will use for this project. In the Cricut Maker, you have the most number of options. you can choose to Cut, Score, Deboss, Wave, Foil, Perforate, Draw or Engrave

Here is an in-depth description of all these options:

Cut Option

The default setting is the Cut option for the Cricut Maker. When this option is selected, whatever you will put on the canvas will be cut when you press 'Make It'. so if your intention is to use another function, be sure to change the setting.

Draw Option

If you want to draw out your designs, you can use this option. When you choose this option, you have to load the Cricut Markers and Pens into the markets sockets provided in the Machine. Remember, the Cricut Maker dose not color your projects.

Scoring Option

The Cricut Maker has a special scoring tip for this function.

This option is useful to make boxes and greeting cards. If you require the project to fold, you can use this tool to score on the lines where the folding is going to take place. this helps your project to have perfect finish.

Deboss Option

Deboss means to press in the material. This is exactly what the deboss tip does.

this function can be used on cardstock and other lightweight materials. this is to beautify your crafts like cards and boxes.

Engrave Option

vilt helps to engrave numerous kinds of materials. This option can be used to engrave monograms and designs on aluminum sheets and other vinyl sheets.

Wave Option

This option is a part of the speciality tips of the Cricut Maker. If you want to make your project with wavy edges, you can use this option. this is ideal for cards, cake toppers, name takes and invites.

Foil Option

this is a decorative option. Can be mostly used to decorate greeting cards, make beautiful monograms and beautify different materials with gold and silver tint. There are speciality gold and silver foil sheets compatible with Cricut Maker which are used for this function.

Perforating Option

This is useful if your project involves making tear out sheets. You can make ticket sheets and vouchers with this function.

Fill

(Fill Icon)

This option is used for printing. this is only available when the cutting linetype is selected. if you choose no fill, it means that only cutting has to done. If you choose the fill option, it means you have to cut as well as print your project. You used your home printer for the printing work and the Cricut Maker for cutting this project.

3. Select All Option

This is a very simple and useful option. If you want to pick up and transfer your whole project at once, you click this option and everything on the canvas will be selected.

4. Editing Option

When you click the Edit Icon, you see a drop down with several options. Cut, copy, paste, duplicate. You can use all these options to cut objects and put somewhere else on the canvas. You can repeat an object or shape you want to cut multiple times in the project.

5. Align Option

(Align Icon)

This option is used to determine where your project will be centered on the canvas. You have different options how to align your project on the canvas.

Align Left: If you choose this option, all the components of the project will be directed from the left side of the canvas. Meaning that the orientation of the project will be left.

Align Correct: If you choose this option, the entire project will be of right orientation.

Center Horizontal: This option is mostly used for photographs. When you choose this, all the components will be oriented horizontally.

Center Vertically: Horizontal: This option aligns all the project components vertical in column form.

Align Top: According to this orientation, the components will be set on the top most part of the canvas.

Align Bottom: If you choose this option, all the components will be aligned to tthe bottom of the canvas.

Center Align: When you select this option, the entire project will be placed in the center of the canvas perfectly.

Distribute: This option is used for spacing between all the elements on the canvas. If you have several objects and cannot space them equally, you select this option to perfectly space all the items. You can space the objects both ways, either horizontally or vertically.

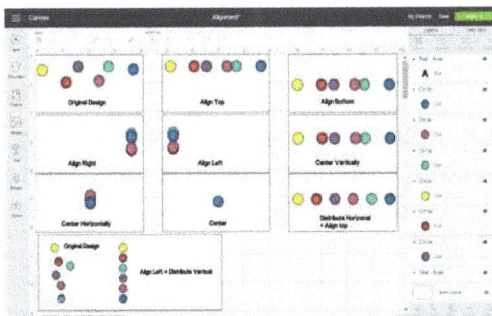

(Different Allignment Options Displayed)

6. Arranging Option

(Arrange Icon)

This function is useful if you have multiple componets on your canvas. Like text, pictures and shapes. This option help you to determine the correct sequence of the componets from top to bottom. with this you will select which component is bottom most and which is top most. Which component goes in the back and which is on the front. You can organize your components according to your design. You have four options. you select each components and arrange them by these four options

Send to Back: Selection of this will make the selected element to transfer to the back of all the other components.

Jump Backward: This option will make the component selected will move one layer back.

Going Ahead : This option will make the component selected to move one layer ahead.

Send to Front: With this option, the component will be placed at the foremost position.

7.Flip Option

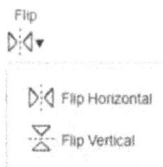

(Flip Icon)

This option creates a reflection of the selected component. There are two options, the image can be flipped either horizontally or vertically.

8. Size Option

This is to size the components of your project. When you click a component and click size and select self, you can manually adjust the size of each component you need to cut. There is a little lock sign that actually locks the dimensions of the components. When you click that lock, it means that you want to change the dimensions.

9.Rotate Option

This option is used to move a certain object towards a certain angle. it can also be used to rotate the object on the canvas at a 180 degree angle or full 360 degree angle.

10.Position Option

This option can be used to position items at a certain place on the canvas. The function is very much like the alignment option but used for more sophetication. this can be used to position single objects through the canvas.

11. Font Option

(Font Icon and Options)

You choose this option to add text to your canvas. Some of the fonts are free to use but for some fonts, you have to pay or subscribe to Cricut Access.

12. Style Option

(Style Icon)

With this option you can turn your fort to either bold, italic or both. Depends on your own choice.

13. Letter space, font space and line space

This option is used to modify your text. The size of the text can be modified, the space between the letters and the space between different words.

14. Alignment Option

(Alignment Icon)

This option is for the text only. If you have a paaragraph or few sentences of text to be cut, you might want to align. The alignment can be either left, center or right.

15. Curve Option

This is a creative option for the text as well. This option has a sliger which is set in the middle. If you move it to the left you will form a rainbow style word alignment. If you move to right, the text will be arranged in the downward direction. If you move to the right most direction, the text will be arranged in a circle form.

16.Advance Option

Advanced

E▮ ▾

E▮	Ungroup To Letters
E▮	Ungroup To Lines
E▮	Ungroup To Layers

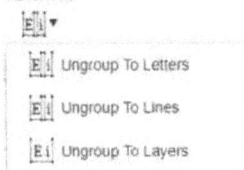

(Advanced Icon)

This option is also for the text on the canvas. This is a drop-down option and you see different options.

Ungroup to Letters: If you want to customize each of your text letter, you can use this option. This option will let you separate every letter in a different layer.

Ungroup to Lines: This option is similar to the ungroup to letters option. The only difference is that it applies to each text sentence or line. If you want to modify each sentence in your paragraph you can use this function.

Ungroup to Layers: This option applies on the multi-layer fonts. These fonts are either available with the Cricut Access subscription or the font usage is individually purchased.

Left Panel

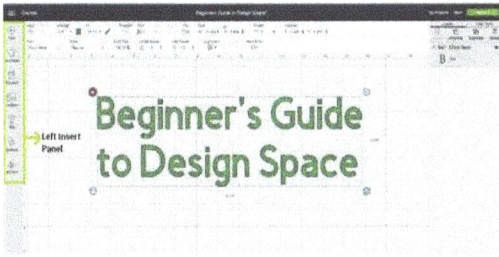

(Left panel of Design Space Highlighted)

In the left panel you can start a new project, view your previous ventures, find photographs and designs for creating a new project. Lets discuss all the options in the panel one by one.

New Button:

to start a new project you click this button and you have a blank canvas.

Template Button:

(Template Display)

The Design Space provides you with a number of generic templates to start a new project. This will serve as a project outline or a mock up. You have alot of options for templates like banners, tags, labels, aprons, T-shirts, shorts etc.

Projects Button:

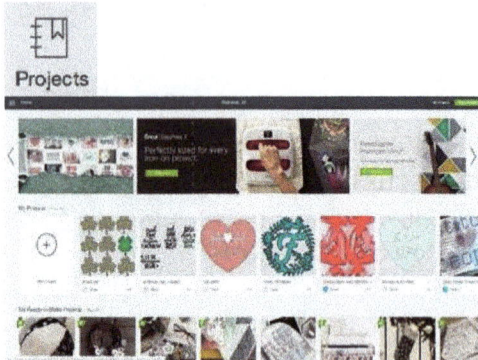

Projects

(Projects Page)

This option has all the projects you have already made. If you have to make a project again, you can easily select the file and press make it. No hassle at all. All the ready made projects from Cricut are also available to make here. If you subscribe to Cricut Access, you will be able to access a wide variety of ready made projects to make.

Images Button:

Images

From here you can find a huge variety of images and photo files to cut. There are images already present with the Design Space. But to gain access to much more images, you will have to subscribe to Cricut Access. The photos and images you will upload yourself as well will appear here.

Text Button:

Text

This is a fairly simple button. You click here and a window appears on the canvas where you can add your text. Then to select the font, style, size, and everything else about the text can be controlled and designed by the top taskbar.

Shapes Button

Shapes

To add simple shapes to your design you click this option. All the basic shapes are given. You can create more intricate designs using these simple shapes. You can adjust the sizes and use more than one shape for your project.

Score Button:

This is a very useful function. This is most useful if you are making cards and boxes which need to be folded after cutting. It is mostly used on light weight materials like the cardstock. When you apply this option on a design, the scoring blade will score along the lines in your design which have to be folded.

Upload button:

Upload

If you want to upload an image for your design you can press upload and select the image from your device. The Design Space software will guide you how to properly upload to use the specific images.

Right Panel – Layers

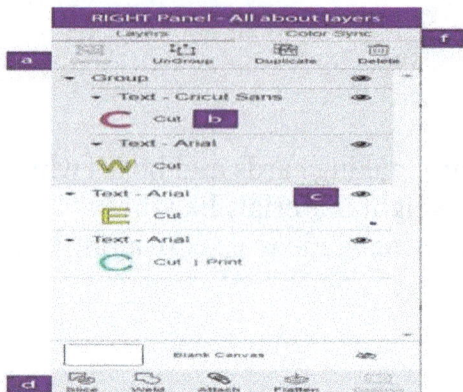

(Right Panel Icons)

This is an interesting part of the project. So, what are layers? Layers in the Cricut world represent each different component or material used in the project on the canvas. So a simple project may have one or two layers and a more complexed project might have five or six layers depending on the design.

You can take an example of a birthday card. So it will have some text, some shapes on the card and the card itself. Now each of these separate component is a layer.

Mostly each component or layer can be edited or modified but there are some files like the JPEG and PNG images, that cannot be edited. The function of the Layers Function is described in detail.

a. Grouping, Ungrouping, Duplicating and Removing

On the layers panel on the top you will find these options.

To Group:

This option is used if you want to make some components of the project as a same layer, or you want those specific components to stick together, you select all the parts and group them together. It can be either only shapes or can be shapes and text. More than one part of the project can be integrated into a single layer.

To Ungroup:

As the name suggests, this means to remore a certain component from a group. Suppose that you want a shape or text to be represented as a separate layer, you choose that component and ungroup it from the other components. Sometimes it is also done to modify or resize a certain part of a group and then can be again regrouped in a single layer.

To Duplicate:

This option creates a copy of an already designed layer. Any layer or design you want to repeat in the same project you cn use this option.

To Delete:

Tis option is very straightforward. If you think a part of the project is not required or has to be removes, the delete option is used.

b. Linetype and Fill

With this option you will choose the linetype for each of the layer. Linetype means that the function to be used to cut the project. Either it has to be cut, or perforated, or scored or be cut in waves aor the project has to be foiled. In this option, you select the function for each layer.

c. Visibility of Layers

On the canvas, each layer has a tiny eye on the side. When you click that eye, the layer will be disappear. A tiny cross will appear at that space. This option is helpful when you want to see each layer separately.

d. Blank Canvas

This option changes the color of the canvas. The canvas is actually white in color. Sometimes you wish to see your designs with a different background. So for that you can change the color of canvas to see the effect. You can use this option on templates as well. If your design is created on templates, you can change the color of templates to see the affect.

e. To Slice, to weld, to attach, to flatten and to contour

All these functions are very useful and are self explanatory from their names.

To Slice:

If you wish to separate a part of text or shape from a design, you select that part or shape and click slice. That part will be separated form the design and you can place is whereever you want to place on the canvas.

To Weld:

To weld is the total opposite of slice. If you want to merge two parts of a design you can use this function. You select both the parts and click weld, and those parts you selected will be merged. This can result in the formation of a whole new design.

To Attach:

This function is like the grouping function, only more stronger. If you select two shapes and click attach both the components will attach and change color. The attached result will take the color of the layer that is on the back. These components will remain intact for the cutting process as well.

To Flatten:

This option is only applicable when you select from no fill to print option. It mans that you have to print then cut design. So if you want to print multiple layers together, you select all of them and then click flatten and can print them together.

To contour:

This option is utilized if you want to leave out parts of the design. Suppose you do not want certain parts of the project. You select those parts and contour them out. The only thing to note is that this option is only available for shapes and designs that has elements which can be contoured or left out.

f. Color Sync

On the design on your canvas, there is a different color representing each material. Now if you need all these shades in your design it is okay. But if you have multiple shades of suppose blue or yellow, you might want to sync them into the same shade. So you click and then drag the color you want to remove and put it on the color you want.

The Main Canvas Area

Here is the space where all the magic takes place. All the functions described in the entire chapter are applied on the canvas. Canvas is the actual place where the designing and creating takes place. We will discuss further the layout of the canvas.

Rulers and Grid of Canvas

The whole canvas is divided into a grid with the x and y axis. The default measurement setting of the grid is in inches. You can also change it to centimeters. The grid gives you an idea and visualization of the project and the size. This grid can be called the visual or digital representation of the Cricut Mats.

Selection

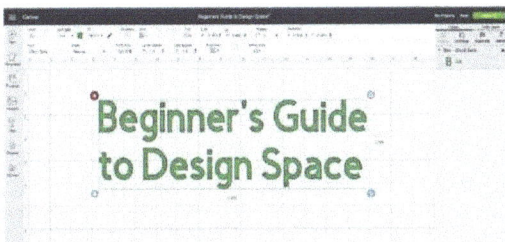

(Main Canvas)

On the canvas each layer is represented with a blue box outlining it. You can select that box and can edit the layer or design in the right panel for layers. On each box on the upper left corner is a tiny cross. If you wnt to delete the layer you can press that button. On the right corner is a curved arrow. You can tilt or rotate the design with the help of this. In the bottom left corner is a small lock. This is supposed to keep the design and image with in proportion. This if, unlocked can make the image disproportional. So it is better not to unlock this option. In the bottom right corner is the option to modify the size of the design.

Cricut Access

A lot of people when starting out with the Cricut Maker get very confused between the Design Space and Cricut Access. There is a simple difference, Design Space is the downloadable software that all current Cricut Machines use for designing and cutting projects. Whereas the Cricut Access is a subscription plan of Cricut. This is a paid service that enables you to use ready made Cricut projects, more than 400 types of texts and 100,000 images. Not only this, when you subscribe with Cricut Access, you get discount of 10 percent on all your Cricut merchandise. Even when you buy sale items you get an additional 10 percent off. As a member of the Cricut Access community, you get a priority status with your orders being jumped up above the non-subscribers. The Cricut Access subscription provides you free shipping for all your orders. It is worth noting that the Design Space provides some free fonts and images as well as some free to use ready to make projects. When you first time register with Design Space, you get a free Cricut Access trial subscription. But you cannot save any image or font of the Cricut Access for use when your subscription is expired. Cricut offers monthly and yearly packages for Cricut Access that can be monthly or yearly renewed. You can directly cancel your subscription at any time.

Chapter 3. Business Ideas for the Cricut Maker

With the advent of the online market places and the popularity of personalized products, small businesses' scope has increased. In this chapter, some ideas to start a business with your creativity and the Cricut Maker are given. There are few universal rules for a good business. Those rules are discussed as follows:

- To start any business a person has to be very patient and very hard working. These are the core rules to become a successful business person. There is no short cut or no easy money scheme. Only hardwork pays off. So if you are thinking of starting your own business, you need to understand that it is going to take time and hardwork to take off. Another golden rule for any business is to create your niche.
- You might have heard the saying, jack of all trades, master of none. This saying applys to most businesses. If you try to do everything at once you will soon become exhausted and loose hope. You need to focus on one thing and create your short term and lon term goals to achive these goals.
- Next most important rule to launch a successful business is to create a product of good quality. People tend to pay a lot of money for good quality product. You can earn more than market price if your product quality is exceptional. Along with being exceptional, your quality should also be consistent. We see a lot of products where the initial quality is good and subsequently it declines.
- In today's age, one of the most important quality of a good business persin is to have networking and marketing skills. The best way to market your product is online and through social media. You have to be very digitally smart to create a successful business online. Market your product on all social media sites. Make tutorials. People tend to buy products which they no about. Create elaborate vedious and tutorials for your products.

With all this wisdom you are perfectly ready to create your very own Cricut Crafts Business. Following are few ideas that might help you stary your business. Best of luck.

Vinyl Stickers and Decals

(Beautiful Decals)

One of the easiest things you can make is vinyl stickers and decals if you own a Cricut Maker. They are in demand, easy to make, and a lot of capital will not be required to start such a business. You can offer to make customized stickers and decals for special occasions as well. Vinyl decals are a very popular thing now a days. You can offer to make decals for the windows. A lot of people these days avoid using curtains for their windows because of dust and allergies. The prefer to cover the windows with decals. You can make different custom sized window decals. A lot of people order for decals for labelling items. For organizing an office or pantry. Youc can create office shelfing decals or pantry organizing decals and sell them online. You can offer creative designs and shapes for these decals. Another idea for decals is different animals and characters for kids. A lot of parents want to decorate their kids rooms with creative options but don't want to spend a lot of money. You can use this as your niche. Create elaborate designs for kids. Cartoon borders for kids room walls. Animal pronts for their windows. Big pictures of colorful animals and plants. Maybe you can offer to make a whole jungle theme for kids rooms. Different thesmes for girls and boys rooms. Thw best thing about this business is that it can be started form the comfort of your own home. The initial investment is also very low. The only thing you will have to work on is your networking and marketing. To get your product to your customers. Work on your networking skills. Market your product everywhere. Use your product yourself. This will be the best publicity. Initially gift your creative product to your friends and family and create awareness about your product in your circle. Positive word of mouth is also very good publicity.

To Get Started:

To start this business, you will need:

- Cricut Maker
- Suitable Vinyl Sheets
- Suitable Mats
- Packaging and posting supplies.

Advantages:

- Low to start the business
- You can start with a small project
- Easy to make
- Do not take a lot of space to setup
- In demand all around the year
- Easy to ship as lightweight

Disadvantages

- The profit rates are low

Custom Mugs, T-Shirts, Tote Bags

(Different Mugs designed with Cricut Maker)

This is a very lucrative business idea. You can make customized and personalized products. You can also make mugs and T-shirts with quirky and exciting phrases and quotes. This can prove to be a very successful business. For this business aswell, networking is the key. If you decide to make t-shirts. Wear those shirts. If someone asks about them, be confident in telling all about those shirts. People love confident people who know what they are talking about. Talk about the quality of material you used. The designs you can offer. How early you can deliver. This is all part of your marketing strategy. A business person is always sure of their product. Know your product inside out. Also use good materials if you are into making clothes. People would pay high prives for good quality fabric. Low quality fabric will not be durable and will create a negative affect for your product. Also be creative with your designs. In todays world people love memes and quirky quotes. Create funny hash tag t-shirts. Be creative with colors. People tend to buy things that are stricking and catchy to the eye.

Similarly if you want to make mugs and cups. Be creative. Use colors. Use the sentiments of people. Your work of art should connect with people. It should make them think about their loved ones. It should make them laugh. It should make them nostalgic. If your art work ignites emothin, if will definitely click with the consumer.

Also with this business, people would want to invest because they will be getting a ready made product. These products make for beautiful gifts aswell. So, you might have high sales in the holiday seasons.

The only drawback to start this business is that the investment cost is high and you will need a bigger space to start this business.

To Get Started:

To start this business, you will need:

- Cricut Maker
- Transfer Vinyl Sheets

- Infusable Ink sheets
- Blank mugs, T-shirts, and tote bags
- Appropriate mats for cutting
- Cricut Easy Press 2
- Packaging and posting materials

Advantages:

- Easy to make
- Market value is higher as it is a finished product
- The profit is higher
- The business has scope all year long

Disadvantages:

- The initial investment is higher
- A bigger space is needed for operations

Giving Cricut Tutorials

A lot of people are investing in the Cricut Maker these days. Though it is easy to use, people find it difficult to read how-to books and manuals. People find it easier to watch a video or get in-person tutorials. You can start a vlog or a tutorial class. You can charge for your tutorial classes. In both ways, you can create an income. By teaching your skill to others you will be able to better your craft aswell as be more confident. A lot of times people who see your vedios or tutorials would want to buy your creative products aswell. This can also be a source of income. You and offer discounts on your tutorial classes such as take one class is 10 dollars but if you book 5 classes you will have to pay 40 dollars. This way you can attract more students to your class. You can advertise your tutorial classes on all social media sites. Another strategy you can use is that you give one class free and the subsequent classes you will charge. People love ti try free classes and tutorials. But if you are successful to get them hooked, then they might aswell join your class. This is not easy but definitely worth it.

To Get Started:

- Cricut Maker
- A video recorder
- A designated space to shoot your videos
- Expertise in editing videos
- All the craft supplies for the crafts you teach

Advantages:

- Can provide tutorials from the comfort of your home
- No initial investment is required
- You get to showcase your creativity

Disadvantages

- Low scope for earnings until you get more students or followers

Party Decorations

(Halowwen Decorations Made by Cricut Maker)

There is a trend to have theme parties these days. People want supplies and decorations like name tags, decorations, give away boxes, cake toppers, etc according to a theme. You can create a business making party decorations and supplies for all kinds of events. All year round, there are birthdays, anniversaries, weddings, bridal, and baby showers. You will never run out of business. This business is for someone who is really creative. Because there is a lot of competition in this field. A lot of event planners charge a lot of money to create theme parties and events. But affordability is a huge issue among people. Everyone wants a lavish party but not all can afford. So you can create personalized party items and sell them at a lower cost than the event planners. This business has a lot of scpe but still a lot of competition is there in this business. The good thing about this business is that the investment costs are low. Also there are personal event all year round so you still can attract a lot of cutomers with your product. This business follows the same rule. If you provide good quality, people will come to you for services. If you are able to offer superior quality than your competitors at a reasonable price, people will pay for your product.

To Get Started:

- Cricut Maker
- Different types of cardstock
- Cutting Mat
- Packaging and postage supplies

Advantages

- Low cost to start the business

Greeting Cards

(Different decorations and Greeting Cards for Chrismas)

Greeting cards are very much in demand, especially during the holiday season. People love to send personalized greeting cards to friends and family. Handcrafted cards have a very personal touch. But not all people have the time or creativity to design and make such greeting cards, so they would want to invest in some handcrafted cards online. This can be started as a seasonal business. The only problem with this business is that it can only flourish in the holiday season. With the digitalization of the whole world, the demand fro cards is declining by the day. However, in the holiday season, there are some people who are old school and still want to follow the old time tradition of sending and exchanging greeting cards, Such old school people will also pay good money for creative and heartfelt greeting cards. So if you plan to start this buiseness, you must create something which connects with the peoples emotions. It has been earlier said in this book to connect with the peoples' emotions. Why is there stress on connecting with people at an emotional level? Because creativity cannot be quantified. Creative businesses always have to connect with peoples' emotions and sensibilities to work.

To Get Started:

- Cricut Machine
- Different types of cardstock
- Decorative materials
- Cutting Mats
- Glue
- Postage and packaging materials

Advantages:

- Easy to make
- The initial investment is low

- Can be sold in bulk
- High rates of profits in the holiday season

Disadvantages:

- The profits can only be gained during holiday seasons

Stuffed Toys

(Creative Stuffed Animal)

Stuffed animals can make beautiful gifts. They can be equally interesting to give to adults as well as children. With the Cricut Maker, you can now easily cut fabric, so this will be a great idea. The Design Space has many free stuffed animal ready made cutting projects. All you have to do is create the finished product out of those designs. You can sell these cuties online for a fair price. This can prove to be a lucrative small business. These stuffed animals are a great gift for babies and kids. Most of the time when we want to gift something to a kid we rely on stuffed animals. The reason being that for other gift items we will have to get the specifics right. For examole if we want to gift a kid clothes, we need to know the exact size. If we want to gift a baby some baby products, we will have to be sensitive about their parents' preferences. In this regard stuffed animals are a great gift. People also want products which are different form the regularly available items. This desire to stand out leads people to invest in handmade and personalized products.

So, for a business, this is a very good idea. These stuffed animals are easy to make and require less time and effort. Fabric and fillings are relatively reasonable to purchase if you buy in bulk. A good idea would be to stick to 2 to 3 styles of stuffed animals when you start your business.

To Get Started:

To get started you will need:

- Cricut Maker

- Suitable Fabric
- Suitable stuffing
- Fabric Grip Mat
- Sewing Machine
- Sewing supplies
- Packing And Posting Supplies

Advantages

- A high rate of profit from buyers if the product is of good quality
- Not a lot of competition
- High purchases during the holiday season

Disadvantages:

- High cost to start the business
- Need a large space for working

Creative Hairbands

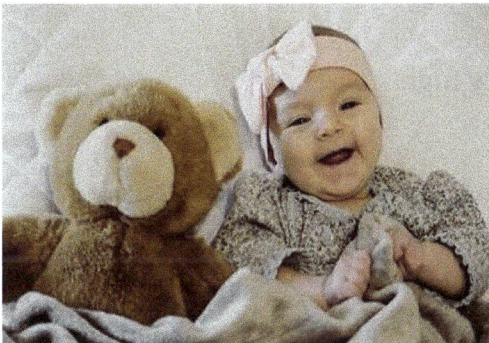

(Kid wearing a headband made with Cricut Maker)

Hairbands are very much in demand right now. Mostly these are popular among toddlers and babies, but women of all ages use them. So these products are in demand among women of all ages. Headbands and head pieces have made a huge comeback these days. For little girls they can prove to be a perfect gift. If you plan to make these headbands, they will prove to be cost effective as less material is used and you can sell it at higher prices because people tend to spend much on their kids and on kids girfting. You can create four or five generic designs and can sell them as a bundle. A good idea would be to select a single design and cut out in four or dive common colors and sell them as a pack. Mothers and aunts of little girls would love to buy such stuff. When creating stuff for toddlers and children be very careful to create stuff with soft materials, if the material will be stiff or hard, they will be useless for kids and no one will buy them.

You can also make headbands for adults as they are very much in fashion. With headbands for girls and ladies you can experiment with more materials and textures. You can even use embelishmets with the headbands. You can even create embellishments with a cricut maker. Headbands with embellishmets can be sold at a higher price.

These are relatively easy to make. Low cost to make and can be stored in a smaller space. Due to them being lightweight, shipping is also easy.

To Get Started:

To get started you will need

- Cricut Maker
- Fabric
- Sewing Machine
- Sewing Supplies
- Packaging and postage supplies

Advantages:

- This product is high in demand
- Sales are high throughout the year
- Scope for profit is high
- The initial cost to start the project is not very high.

Disadvantages:

- A lot of competition already there in the market place.

Keychains

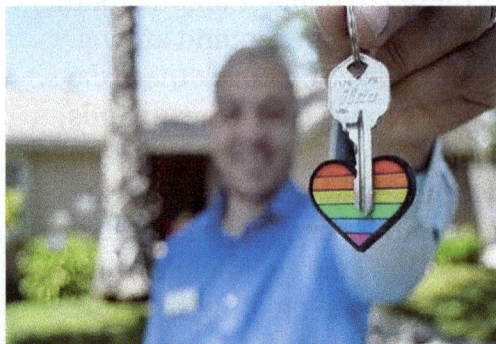

(A Creative Keychain)

With the Cricut Maker, it is possible to cut materials such as leather and wood. This allows you to create unique keychains. People are very fond of fun and quirky key chains. Keychains can be sold online for a fair price. The good thing about keychans is that it can be sold to men and women both. They are not gender restrictive. With keychins also, people want to stand out with their unique style. If you want to create designs for men and women both, you have to target at both of them. One way is to create unisex designs and the other way is to create two different types of products. This depends entirely on you, how you want to target your consumer and what works for you. Whatever style you choose, you will have to be extremely creative. One thing is worth mentioning, leather is a very popular material for keychains. This also gives a very sophisticated effect. Leather products can be sold at a higher price. So, you might consider making leather keychains.

To Get Started:

To get started, you need:

- Cricut Maker
- Strong Grip Cutting Mat
- Knife blade
- Materials for the keychain (wood or leather)
- Keyrings
- Packaging and postage supplies

Advantages

- Easy to create
- Can be sold for a reasonable price
- Easy to ship as it is a lightweight product

Disadvantages:

- The startup cost is relatively high.
- The materials for the keychain are expensive

Paper Flower Bouquets

(Bouqet made of paper Flowers)

Real flowers are very expensive. The tend to wilt soon as well. But you need flower bouquets for all occasions and especially for gifting. Flowers are a huge part of weddings. Everyone wants their wedding to look like a fairytale wedding. But sometimes our pockets don't allow that kind of luxury. In weddings people look for alternatives of real flowers and paper crafted flowers are a decent substitute. Paper flowers, if created correctly, look verymuch like real flowers. People would invest in real looking paper flowers. If you can create a good quality product, this business can gain a lot of profits. The condition for success in this business is quality and price. If you can provide an exceptional quality at a competitive price, your business can take off. The drawback of this business is the level of concentration it requires to create each flower. The amount of work required to create even a single flower. For such kinds of bouquets to look real, each flower has to be cerated by connecting separate petals. This requires a high level of precision and a lot of patience to create each flower. You need to be very cerative to design a whole bouquet. Sometimes when you create a flower, it looks very beautiful individually but doesn't look as appealing when a part of a bouqet. So, it is important to actually create beautiful flowers as well as intricate designs for the bouquet. So, if you are not passionate enough for this level of perfection, this business might not be for you. But, if you are enthusiastic about something like this, go for it by all means.

To Get Started:

To get started you will need:

- Cricut Maker
- Standard and Light Grip Mat
- Crepe paper
- Thin and thick cardstock
- Different colored paper
- glue

- flower wire
- wirecutter
- scissors
- Packing Materials
- Postage Materials

Advantages

- The margin for profit is high
- This is a booming business, and there is not a lot of competition

Disadvantages:

- Challenging to ship due to size and fragility
- A high-quality product is required
- Time-consuming to create individual bouquets

Chapter 4. DIY Cricut Maker Projects

Pantry Project

Now, by this point, it has already been established that you are a creative person, but are you a super organized person as well? If the answer to this question is yes, you would love to have your pantry organized. And what pantry can be organized without labels? Worry no more; here you have a simple step by step project to create labels for your pantry jars and bottles. The following DIY project is about kitchen labels. These labels go well with clear canisters as well as solid-colored ones. One tip to make the labels would be that we do not design labels for patterned boxes and containers. This will create an untidy finish. It is also recommended that you should have uniform containers for organizing. This gives a clean look and motivates you to keep the pantry organized because of its visual effect on your mind.

In this tutorial, label making is directed towards making them for the kitchen containers. But you can use the same tutorial to create labels for other organization projects as well. You can label your crafts closet and containers with these labels. If you are a teacher, you might want to create labels for your supply closet. In short, the possibilities are unlimited. Let us get started with this straightforward and basic project to create labels.

(Kitchen Jars with Cricut Labels)

- Cricut Maker Project Level: Easy (Beginner)
- Time: Start to finish – 2 hours approximately.
- Materials and Supplies:
  - Cricut Maker Machine
  - Premium Fine Point Blade
  - Cricut Removable Vinyl
  - Cricut Transfer Tape
  - Design Space Software
  - Cricut Access
  - Cricut Toolkit

- Cricut Scraper Tool
- Cricut Standard Grip Mat
- Instructions:

1. First, you must have a cleared, decluttered space whenever you start any project. Then you collect all the supplies you are going to require in the project. Only after that, you must start your project.
2. Next, measure out what size you require for labels. This step is essential. It will help if you determine what size labels you want for your jars and containers. If you skip this step, there are chances that the labels would come out larger or smaller than necessary. So please do not miss this step.
3. Next, open your Design Space on your laptop or any other device you prefer to use.
4. Go to the canvas page. On the left panel, click the New option. Now, you will have a clear canvas.
5. After this, you have two options, either select from the already given projects and customize them according to your requirement, or you do it manually. It is often suggested that you make your first few projects by selecting the already made projects. But here, the manual method is explained.
6. The first step will be to choose the template. You easily click the template button and choose the appropriate template which will be for labeling.
7. Next, go to the text. Choose your preferred font and type out all the labels. Adjust the font size.
8. When you are satisfied with your labels, click the "Make It" button.
9. After clicking the 'Make It" button, the software might align all the labels differently than you typed out. Do not worry. This alignment will be to use the materials most effectively.
10. After this, the software will give you commands to arrange everything in order before it starts cutting.
11. For this project, you will install the Premium Fine point blade.
12. Next, you will stick the vinyl sheet to the cutting Mat.
13. When all is adequately aligned, install the Mat to the Cricut Maker. It will start cutting now.
14. You must wait till the Cricut completes cutting.
15. Next is the fun part. The process of weeding. First, you take out the Mat from the Cricut Maker. Remove your vinyl from the grip mat. Use a hook tool to weed out all the excess space, only leaving the text. Be incredibly careful because this process needs attention and precision. Before starting to weed, you can also cut the labels in rectangles or the required shape. It will take time and concentration to weed all the labels.
16. Now only the text and the backing piece of vinyl are left. All the unnecessary vinyl has already been weeded.

17. Next comes the transfer tape. Carefully cut the transfer tape according to the size of the labels. Now peel off one side of the transfer tape and push it down on the label. Use the Cricut scraper tool to press on the transfer tape properly. Repeat this process with each label.
18. This must be done with precision to give a neat finish.
19. The next step is to carefully pull back the transfer tape from the backing material. Ensure that the entire text of the label comes off with the transfer tape when you pull up.
20. Next, stick the label directly to the container. Before pressing it hard, check that the placement is correct. When you are sure of the placement, use the Cricut scraping tool to press the label against the jar or bottle for firm adherence.
21. Repeat the process with each label.

Outdoor Welcome Mat

A thing about crafters and creative people is that they have this desire to showcase their work. They love praise. They want their work to be displayed for people to see and appreciate. If you are one of those, this project is for you. What else is better than placing your piece of art right at your doorstep. As soon as someone is about to enter your house, they will see this unique piece and will stop to ask where you got it from, and you can proudly announce that this is my creation. This project is a simple and elegant welcome mat to be placed outside your doorstep. You can modify this project and make an elaborate piece. But for beginners, it is recommended to first get practice with the easier stuff. Easier stuff will be made quickly and boost your sense of achievement. When you complete a few easy projects successfully, you will be confident enough to graduate to the next level. For now, you might want to try this simple DIY Cricut project.

- Cricut Maker Project Level: Easy (Beginner)
- Time: Start to finish- 3 hours approximately
- Materials and Supplies:
- Cricut Maker
- Standard Grip Cutting Mat
- Premium Fine Point Blade
- Cricut Removable Vinyl
- Cricut Toolset
- Navy Blue Craft paint (weather resistant)
- Foam paintbrush (with round tip)
- Coir Rug
- Instructions

1. It is always useful to clean up your space before starting any project. Just clear up your space and collect all the materials and supplies you would need for the project.
2. First, measure your Mat and determine the size of the text you want to place on the Mat.
3. Open Design Space on your laptop or the device of your choice. Go straight to the canvas and start a new project.
4. Next, click the text button. The text toolbar will appear on the top of the page.
5. You can choose your favorite font, adjust the size, and type your text. It can be something as simple as hello.
6. Next, you will click the Make it button. With this command, the software will guide you through the entire cutting process.
7. For this project, you will insert the Premium Fine tip blade.
8. Next, stick the vinyl to the cutting Mat.
9. Install the Mat to the Cricut Maker and wait for the cutting to be done.

10. Once the cutting is done, take the vinyl sheet off the Mat and start weeding.
11. Weed out tur letters from the vinyl using the weeding tools from the Cricut Toolbox. Leave the rest of the vinyl sheet intact.
12. When you are done with weeding, take off the vinyl from the backing paper and set the vinyl sheet on the Mat where you want to place the text.

(Mat with vinyl sheet set as a stencil)

13. This will act as a stencil.
14. Now use the craft paint and the foam brush to color withing the stencil.
15. After the painting is complete, wait for a while before removing the vinyl.
16. Waiting for 10 to 15 minutes will be sufficient.
17. Now let the paint dry. It will take a while, and then your Mat is ready to use.

Decorative Birdhouse

This birdhouse project is a beautiful one. This birdhouse project is included in the free Design Space projects. This is a ready-made project with all the settings and measurements in place. You must select this project and click "Make it." But be careful; if you are a beginner, you might want to try a few more projects before you attempt this one. This is an advanced project. For this birdhouse, more than two different materials are used in the making. The base materials will be chipboard. Three different cutting tools are also used. This birdhouse can be kept for yourself as decoration. It is also ideal for gifting.

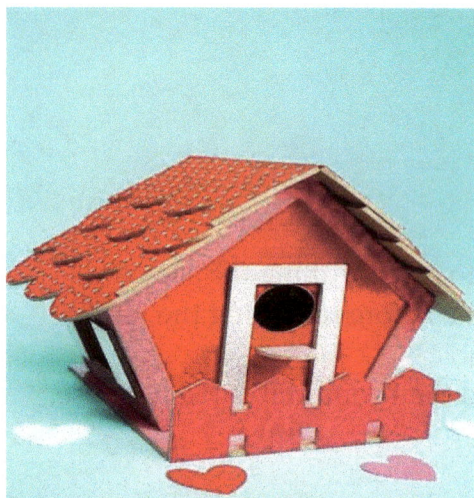

(A decorative birdhouse)

- Cricut Maker Project Level: Advanced (Competent)
- Time: Start to finish 4 hours
- Materials and Supplies:
  - Cricut Maker Machine
  - Easy Press 2 (Cricut)
  - Hooked weeding tool
  - White glue
  - Damask patterned chipboard
  - Glittered vinyl (Silver)
  - Cricut chipboard
  - Fusible fabric(red)
  - premium permanent vinyl in pink and red
  - Adhesive foil (red)
  - Knife blade
  - Fine point blade
  - Rotary blade

- Instructions:
1. For every project, it is most important to first have a clean, clutter-free space.
2. Then collect all the materials, supplies, and all the different blades you will require.
3. Once all of this is done, turn on your laptop or device with design space and start. As this project is already present in the Design Space, you will not have to design in this project.
4. Just go to the projects and choose the Birdhouse Design and click 'Make It."
5. Now as simple as it seems, to complete the whole project will take some time and expertise.
6. When you click the Make its option, the cutting process can be started.
7. The software will give you instructions regarding the materials and blades to be used.
8. According to the instructions, this project will be cut into 20 mats.
9. First, you install the Knife blade and cut the Demask Patterned chipboard as Mat one.

(Cricut maker during the cutting process)

10. Now for mats 2 and 3, you will use the chipboard. The design space will also instruct for multiple passes for compete cutting. You can follow the instruction to fully complete the cutting for each material sheet or Mat.
11. After cutting the chipboards, the blade will be changed to a fine point blade. With this blade, the three types of Sheet will be cut:
- Adhesive foil
- Premium permanent vinyl both sheets
- Glitter vinyl sheet
12. The standard cutting mat will be used for these cuttings.

(Cutting the Adhesive foil)

13. Next, the blade must be changed to the rotary blade. With these, the fusible fabric cutouts will be easily cut.
14. This step will end the cutting process. You can now put away the Cricut maker. And start weeding with the hooked weeding tool.
15. When all the wedding is done, you will start assembling the project. The instructions for that are given in the project file.
16. First, you will transfer all the vinyl cuttings appropriately to the chipboard cuttings.
17. Transfer the fusible fabric to the rooftop cuttings with the help of the Cricut Press 2. Heat the easy press to 300 degrees Fahrenheit and keep the cupboard and fabric under the press for 30 seconds. Let it cool down before use.

(Heating the Easy Press 2)

18. When all the projects are ready, join them together with the help of white glue.

(Completing the Birdhouse)

Cricut Maker Mug for Grandpa

Grandparents are such a blessing. They are like a second set of parents, only gentler and kinder. Being with one's grandparents is always an enriching experience. Sometimes we need to let them know how much we love them. This project is about creating a gratitude mug for grandpa. The tutorial topic is about grandpa, but you can use this basic tutorial to create many different mugs. You just must follow the same instructions and create your designs. This is one of the easiest projects in this book. Also, it takes significantly less time to be completed. Also, personalized mugs can be gifted. In the previous chapter, selling personalized mugs is also given as a business idea.

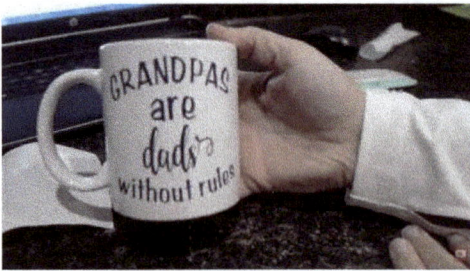

(Competed Mug for Grandpa)

- Cricut Maker Project Level: Easy Beginner
- Time: Start to finish- 1 hour 30 minutes
- Materials and Supplies:
- Cricut Maker Machine
- Standard Grip Mat
- Vinyl
- Cricut Scraping tool
- Measuring tape
- Blank Mug (can be white or any other color)
- Scissors
- Instructions:
1. Clear up all your working space. Turn on your laptop or device where you will design the project.
2. Collect all the materials necessary for the project.
3. Open the design space and insert the design or text you want to transfer on your mug.
4. Here we selected some text.
5. Upload your design.
6. Now, as we are creating vinyl for the mug, we need to adjust the text to be placed easily on the mug's curved surface.

7. You can even select a design from the images or make projects available in the design space. It is more fun to create your designs, though.
8. Now use the rotate option to align the text according to the mug. You can also measure the mug beforehand and size the text accordingly.

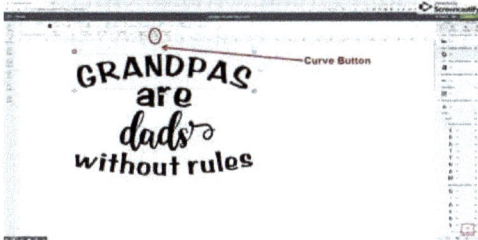

(The curve button)

9. When you are satisfied with your design, click the attach button on the right-side layers panel. This is so that all the text is cut together when cutting in the Cricut Maker.
10. Next, you unlock the design. If you do not unlock the design, you might not be able to customize it.
11. Adjust the dimensions of the design. A standard-sized mug should have a 5cm-by-5cm design that will look good.

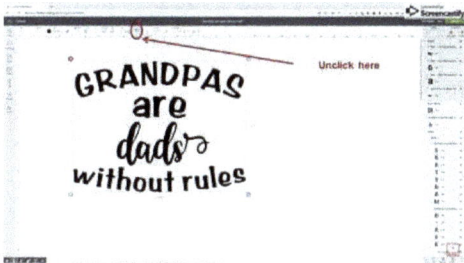

(The unlock Icon)

12. When you are satisfied with your design, click 'Make It".
13. Follow the instructions and set up the Mat and viny carefully, and let the project be cut.

(The Prepare screen before cutting)

14. Once the project is cut, weed it with the help of weeing tools.
15. Clean your mug of any dust particles.
16. Now prepare the transfer tape of the same size as the design.
17. Please take off the backing from the transfer tape and attach it to the vinyl. Press to remove all air bubbles. You can also use a scraping tool to smooth the transfer tape.
18. Carefully remove the transfer tape with the design.
19. Now your beautiful mug is ready.

Coasters

(Colorful coasters)

Everyone roams around their house with a hot cup of tea or coffee and places it on their furniture, ruining your wooden tables and marble counters. For this purpose, we need coasters. And if you are a creative person, you would want to design and create your coasters. Cricut sells coasters in two designs, one square, and one circle. These are sold as a pack of four. The circle and square ones are slightly different. The circle ones are ceramic, and the square ones are ceramic on the top and have a cork backing. To design and create these coasters, the method is the same. In this project, we are going to design the coasters with Transfusible Ink Transfer sheets. These are a product of Cricut, these are like heat transfer sheets, but the difference is that they transfer colored Ink onto the surfaces, and the Ink is transferred to the product by applying heat. The finished products give a watercolor effect. The design space has quite a few patterns and quotes for these coasters. You can create four similar coasters or can choose four different designs from the Design Space. This project is easy to make but does involve some level of expertise, especially to transfer the Ink onto the coasters. Also, you need a bit of practice to use Easy Press 2.

Let us start this project and create some beautiful coasters.

Cricut Maker Project Level: Intermediate

- Time: Start to finish – 2 hours
- Materials and supplies
- Cricut Maker Machine
- Ceramic Coasters by Cricut
- Standard grip mat
- Infusible ink transfer sheets
- Cricut Easypress with a heat mat
- Fine point blade

- Instructions:
1. Clear up all the working space. Set your laptop or device. Keep all the materials near you.
2. Once you enter Design Space, you will start a new project.
3. Go to images and search for round coasters.

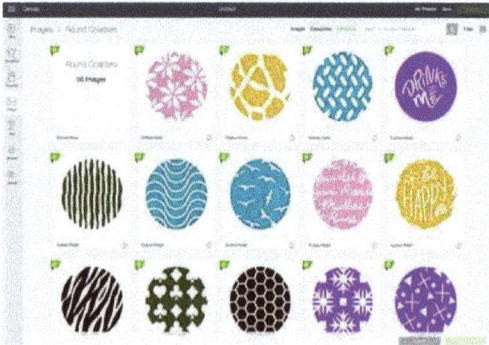

(Image selection for coasters)

4. You will get several designs in the library. If you are a beginner, it is always wise to choose pictures and projects in the Design Space. The sizes of the projects are compatible with Cricut products. In this project, we are using Cricut coasters. If you choose a project from the design space library, the sizing will be proper. However, if you want to design your project, the coasters' size is 3.5 inches by 3.5 inches.
5. After choosing the design, you can duplicate it. If you are making four coasters, you replicate the image four times and select the same color so that all coasters can be cut on the same Ink Infusible Sheet.
6. You can align the design according to your desire. Also, by alignment, you can save your infusible ink sheets.
7. Next click 'Make It.' After that, on the Prepare Screen, select the Infusible Ink Transfer Sheet as your custom material.

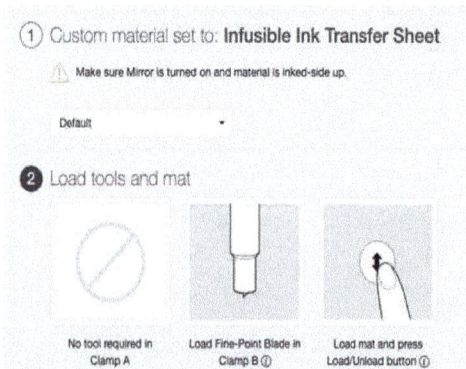

(Instructions and settings for the Infusible Ink Sheet)

8. Do not forget to mirror the design if you have text on it. If you just have a pattern on it, it will not necessarily matter. But the text must be mirrored. For some designs, to appear the same as the screen, it is best to mirror the image before cutting.
9. The blade used for these sheets is the fine point blade. Check that this blade is installed.
10. Prepare your Standard Grip Cutting Mat and the Infusible Ink Transfer sheet. The transfer sheet with liner side down on the Cutting Mat. Do not be worried if you feel that the colors appear dull on the Sheet. These colors appear very vibrant on the finished product.

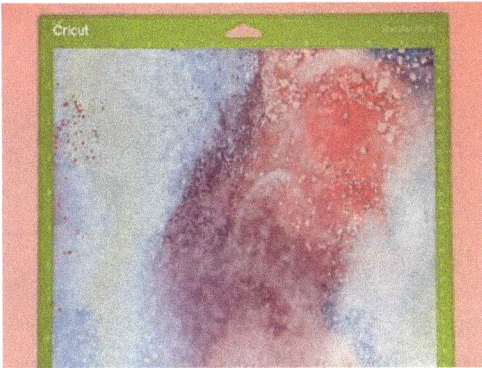

(The Infusible Ink sheet adhered to the Cutting Mat)

11. Next, the cutting of the project takes place. Insert the Mat into your machine and wait for the project to be cut.
12. Remove the Sheet from the Mat. The Infusible ink sheet has two sheets. Remove the thin Sheet. Now you will be left with the Sheet with the Ink.
13. Next, weed out all the negative space.
14. Now cut all the coaster cuttings separately.

(Blank coasters and Transfusible Ink Cutouts)

15. Now prepare the Easy Press 2 for the design transfer to the coasters.
16. Follow the heat instructions on the Infusible Ink Sheet.
17. You will heat the Easy Press to 400 degrees Fahrenheit.

18. Next, you will align your design and coaster for the transfer of Ink.
19. First, place the heat mat and place plain cardstock over it so that it is not damaged. Then put the weeded design with the Ink side facing up. After that, place the coaster, the shiny side placed in the Ink sheet. Set the coaster directly on the design. Now put the butcher paper on the coaster that comes with the Ink Transfer sheet.

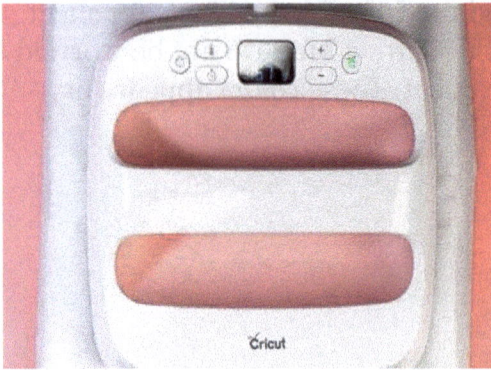

(Easy Press 2)

20. Now apply the Easy Press 2 for 4 minutes.
21. Remove the Easy Press 2 and put it on its bracket.
22. The coasters are ready but do not pick them up with your bare hands because these are too hot.
23. If you want to pick them up, use an oven mitt.
24. Do not place on wood or plastic surface; place some Sheet to place the coasters face up.
25. Your beautiful coasters are ready.

Wooden Earrings.

Jewelry is every girl's weakness. There are very few girls who do not wear jewelry or do not like jewelry. Customized jewelry is a creative way to express yourself. With the Cricut Maker, you can cut and shape several different materials. The main difference with the Cricut Explore is its ability to cut thicker and heavier materials. It would help if you had a ticker and more sturdy material to create jewelry. So, the Cricut Maker is ideal for jewelry creation. You can design all kinds of pieces, like necklaces, chunky rings, earrings, bracelets, anklets, etc., with the Cricut Maker. Personalized and handmade jewelry make for unique gifts. You can gift your loved one's pieces according to their unique personalities. And with Cricut Maker, you can create jewelry with more than 100 materials. In this tutorial, we discuss a specific pinecone earring made from wood veneer, which is wood, sliced into very thin layers and then adhered together with strong glues to make it stronger and more durable. This is an easy-to-follow step by step tutorial to create beautiful earrings.

(Pinecone Earrings)

- Cricut Maker Project Level: Intermediate
- Time: Start to finish – 2 hours
- Materials and Supplies:
  - Cricut Maker
  - Earring hooks
  - Jump rings
  - Jewelry pliers
  - Deep cut blade
  - Cricut Wood Veneer (light brown)
  - Cricut Wood Veneer (dark brown)
  - Strong Grip Mat
  - Cricut Scraper
  - Cricut Tweezers
  - Cricut Brayer
- Instructions:

1. Before starting any project, it is always best to declutter the working space. Collect all the materials required to complete the project
2. Turn on the Design Space. For this project, you will have to make a Cricut Access purchase. If you are a subscribed member, this will be available for you for free.
3. Select the Pinecone Earring Svg and pay for the design.
4. Upload the design.

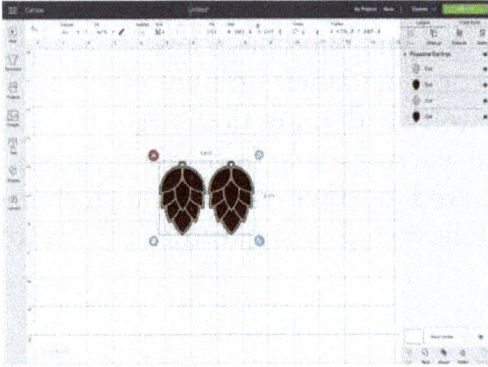

(The canvas display of Pinecone earrings)

5. A reasonable size for such earrings will be 2.5 inches tall. If you want to change the size, you can easily do it on the Edit Toolbar.
6. When you are done editing, click 'Make It.'
7. When you enter the Prepare Screen, you will see that this project will be cut on two mats. It means that this project has two layers or two parts. Do not make any changes on the Prepare screen.

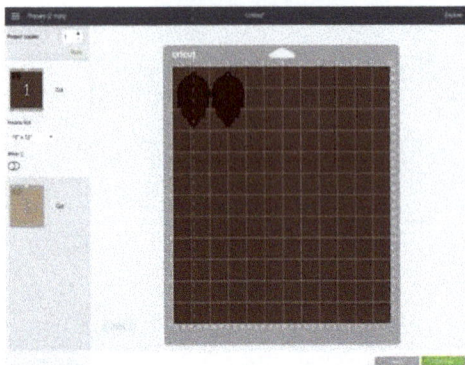

(Prepare screen)

8. On the Make screen, select your custom material to be a wood veneer.
9. Next, check the blade in your machine; it should be a deep cut blade.
10. Prepare your material. Place the veneer on the Strong Grip mat. Use a brayer for the proper adhesion. If it is needed, you can fix it with tape.
11. Now let the first layer cut.
12. Next, prepare the other Sheet to be cut in the same way.

13. When both sheets are ready, peel off the wood from the Mat.
14. Weed out the cuttings from the wood.
15. Now assemble your earrings. Align the two layers, darker at the back and lighter in the front.
16. Connect them with a jump ring and close it with the pliers. Now connect with the fishhooks, taking care that you attach the fishhook in the correct direction.
17. Your beautiful earrings are ready to wear. You can either use them yourself or gift them to your loved ones.

(Wood veneer cutouts)

Felt Bows

This is also a ready-made project. We will make these creative and beautiful bows together. These bows are easy and straightforward to cut as the whole project with instruction is being used. The assembly process is time-consuming and will require more concentration. During the assembly of these bows, you must be very careful. The glue will stick the bow together, and it takes a while for the fabric to fully attach with glue. If you do not work with patience, this assembly may become very messy. And messy projects do not give a good impression.

The bows you will create are usually used for decoration. You can sow or glue a felt boy to a baby hairband.

These bows can be glues to blank pins to create beautiful hair embellishments for little girls. They can even be glued to scrunchies to create decorative hair ties.

In the following project, three different styles of od bows are included. With step-by-step instructions, the project is relatively easy to follow.

(Finished Felt Bows)

- Cricut Maker Project Level: Intermediate
- Time: Start to Finish – 2 hours
- Materials and Supplies:
- Cricut Maker
- Rotary blade for fabric
- Hot glue gun
- Strong Grip Mat
- Cricut Felt material of different colors
- Scissors
- Instructions:
1. Clear up the working space. Turn on your laptop or device with a design space.

2. Start a new project.
3. For this project also you will need to purchase an image from Cricut Access. You will have to pay a small price if you want to buy an individual image, but it will be easy to access if you are subscribed to Cricut Access.
4. Choose the Felt Bow SVG.
5. Next, upload the template on the Design Space. It will appear on the Canvas.
6. You can now resize and change the color of each bow on the template.
7. This is ready to make the project, so remember not to unlock it. The individual bows are already attached.
8. If you want to cut the entire project with the same color and same material, you can unlock the design. Then attach all the components and cut on the same piece of felt. However, in this tutorial, we are making each bow on a separate piece of felt.
9. When you are satisfied with your design, click the 'Make It' button.
10. Next comes the Prepare screen. Each bow appears on a separate mat.
11. On the Make screen, choose the correct material. Since we are using the Cricut Felt, the Mat's size will not have to be adjusted.
12. Check that the rotary blade has been installed in the Cricut Maker. This blade is especially for fabric and is exclusive to the Cricut Maker.
13. Next, prepare the felt on the Strong Grip Mat.
14. Install the Mat into the machine and let the cutting be done.

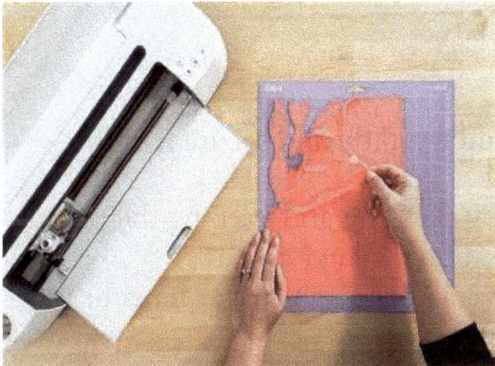

(Removing the negative area)

15. Remove the felt from the Cricut Mat. It will leave behind all the components of the bow.
16. Repeat the same procedure with other felt sheets.
17. Separate all the cut pieces for the bows.
18. Now when you have got all the cutouts, assemble the bows.

(Assembling the bows)

19. Take the first cut out, fold one side to the center, and stick it with the glue. Repeat the same with the other side. You will have the basic bow shape.
20. Turn over the bow and stick it to the larger bow cut out with the glue gun.

(Simple Bow Assembly)

21. Now wrap around the thin cutout in the middle tightly and secure it at the back.
22. The other bow is also assembled similarly by stacking and sticking the pieces from bigger to smaller. Then secure them with the center cutout.
23. The next bow is cut in a way that it has four corners. Each corner must be brought into the middle and glued in the center.

(Bow With four Edges)

24. Next, you will wrap around the center cutout and glue it securely. At the back, you will attach the ribbon cutout.
25. You can also mix and match these bows or can make them in solid colors.
26. These bows can be used for decorations for kids and holiday gift packaging. These bows will be most useful to glue on little girls' headbands, hairclips, and hair ties.

Baby Onesie (Everyday Iron-On)

Babies are the cutest creatures on earth. They have the tiniest hands and the most innocent faces. It is always so wonderful to create stuff for kids. It is prevalent among parents these days to make their kids wear onesies with exciting quotes and quirky designs. If you are one of those parents who enjoy following trends, then this project will interest you. In this DIY project, we will be creating a customized onesie for a baby. Whenever you are making stuff for infants and kids in general, use the right quality materials. Especially fabric. Kids have extremely sensitive skins. They cannot wear materials that are not pure. It is best to use good, quality cotton-based material for kids.

Baby onesies are a great gift idea. With the Cricut Maker, you can create personalized gifts for your loved ones. Cricut sells onesies for babies so that you can use them. They are compatible with their easy iron-on sheets. You can also use regular blank onesies for your projects. They work equally well. This project will create a baby onesie with an iron-on design created by the Cricut Maker. One thing about iron-on designs is that you always must mirror them before sending them to cut. Otherwise, the design orientation will be the opposite of what you see on screen.

With all the useful instructions in mind, let us start our baby project.

(Iron On design Onesie)

- Cricut Maker Project Level: Easy (Beginner)
- Time: Start to finish – 1 hour

- Materials and Supplies:
  - Cricut Maker
  - Cricut Onesie
  - Easy Press Mini
  - Hook weeding tool
  - Cricut Everyday Iron-on Sheet
  - Standard Grip Mat
  - Lint roller
  - Bucher paper
  - Scissors
- Instructions:

1. Clear up your working space. Collect all the materials you will require for the project. It is always less time consuming if you have a clean working space.
2. Open design space. This is a simple tutorial for a onesie. Start a new project.
3. Open the images and select a cute animal image. Upload it on the canvas. Fill it with the checkered background so that the outline of the image is cut. Adjust the size of the image.
4. Now from the text icon, add text to your design area. You can select the font, size, and style of the text.
5. Now align the text with the image. Set the proportions so that the image and text look compatible.
6. Now select the image and text and attach them with the attach button in the right panel.
7. Now adjust the size of the design.
8. As it is a baby onesie, the right size would be 3 inches in width and 4 inches in length.
9. When all is determined, the press makes it.
10. See on the prepare screen that only one Mat is shown.
11. Then on the made screen, select the Everyday Iron-on Sheet. Also, mirror the project.
12. Prepare the Cutting Mat and the iron-on Sheet.
13. Now let the project be cut.
14. When the project is cut, remove the iron-on Sheet from the Mat and cut around the design edges with scissors.
15. Now weed out the negative space with the weeding hook tool.
16. Now, prepare the blank onesie. Clear all the dirt and dust on it with the lint roller.
17. Place the design on the onesie. Align it properly.
18. Put a butcher paper on the design.
19. Turn on the Easy press mini to the recommended temperature for cotton.

20. Now iron on the design. Keep ironing for about a minute so that the design is fully transferred.
21. Your cute onesie is ready. Either you made it for your baby or created it to gift it to someone; this is one of the most satisfying projects you will ever make.

Infusible Ink T-Shirt

T-shirts are always in fashion. Sometimes you want to personalize your shirts with your creative style. Sometimes you come across such quotes or saying that you want to say out loud. What better expression would be other than wearing those quotes. Personalized T-Shirts say so much about your personality and individuality. If you are an expressive and creative person, you would surely be interested in creating your shirts. You can do this easily with a Cricut Maker and beautiful Infusible Ink Transfer Sheets. Infusible Ink Transfer sheets come in beautiful patterns and designs. There are soft and pastel-colored designs, as well as vibrant colors and patterns as well. When you see an Infusible Ink Transfer sheet, you would feel that it has dull colors. But when it transfers on materials, it has very fresh and vibrant colors.

This is a relatively easy project. But the only hurdle will be the Ink transfer part. If you are a beginner, this part can be a little difficult and messy for you. Also, another thing is handling Easy Press 2. This heats up fast and too high temperatures. Be incredibly careful while handling it. If you have children, you might want them to be out of the working area when dealing with heat.

With all these instructions, let us start making our beautiful T-Shirt.

(A fun shirt made with Cricut maker)

- Cricut Maker Project Level: Easy (Beginner)
- Time: Start to finish- 2 hours
- Materials and Supplies:
- Cricut Maker
- Easy Press 2
- Heat mat
- Light Grip Mat

- Infusible Ink transfer sheet (Shaylee pattern)
- Scissors
- Cricut Blank White T-Shirt
- Cardstock
- Butcher paper
- Lint roller
- Hook weeding tool
- Instructions:

1. Clear up your working space. Collect all the things you would require for your project.
2. Open design space. Select a new project. The design shown in the picture is available as a ready-made project by the name of the rainbow is my favorite color. You can pay a small price and select that from Images as an SVG. Or you can design your shirt as well.
3. If you want to use the same file, you buy it and then upload it. The file is of the accurate proportions for a medium-sized shirt. So, there will be no need to adjust the size and straight ahead to the Make it button.
4. But in case you want to make your design, you add some text. Edit the fonts, size of the text. You can also write text in three or four lines and change each line's font and size to make it more interesting.
5. You can add basic shapes to your design and set them around your text.
6. Or you can add an image to your design
7. After setting up your design, check the proportions and alignment, and remember to attach the text and images to print the design all in one layer.
8. When it is attached, you can determine the size of the design.
9. For a medium-sized shirt, the right size would be 6 inches by six-inch, or if it is a larger design, it can also be 6 inches by 8 inches in size.
10. When you are satisfied with your design, press make it.
11. Next, check the prepared screen that everything is on the same layer.
12. Go to the Make screen and be sure to mirror your design.
13. Choose Infusible Ink for your material.
14. Be sure to use a fine point blade.
15. Set your Mat with the infusible ink sheet. Set the Sheet according to the instructions given on the box.
16. Let the project be cut.
17. Remove the Infusible Ink Sheet from the cutting Mat.
18. With the hook tool, weed out the negative space. Be extremely careful in weeding the project.
19. Cut out the design from the Sheet.
20. Prepare the T-Shirt for the project. Clean it with a lint roller.

21. Put cardstock in the middle of the t-shirt layers. This is because the color from the Infusible Ink sheets can be transferred to the other side of the shirt and ruin the design.
22. Place the Infusible ink sheet on the t-shirt. Try to align in the center.
23. Place butcher paper on the Sheet.
24. Heat the Easy Press 2 according to the instruction for cotton material.
25. Press the design on the t-shirt for two minutes.
26. Now, wait for a while before taking out the cardstock.
27. Let the Ink dry for 3 to 5 minutes.
28. The colors appear to be very vibrant when printed on the material. Otherwise, the sheets seem to be very dull.
29. Do not worry if you feel the sheets are dull; they are highly pigmented.

Tote Bags

Another very fashionable accessory is a tote bag. You can make your style statement with cool, personalized tote bags. Tote bags with creative patterns and quotes are real in things these days. These are suitable for a nice picnic day on a beach with friends. Or you can gift your friends a nice creative tote bag with their favorite quote or their favorite-colored design. They are straightforward to make and are useful. In this project, we are going to use Heat Transfer vinyl on a tote bag. This is a simple project, and you can make it in many ways you please. You can make a customized tote bag with other materials as well Cricut has Glitter Iron On sheets for a blingy finish. If you are into bling, you should try making the tote bag with a glitter sheet. Another option to create a beautiful watercolor effect on the tote bag is to use Transfusible Ink Transfer sheets. You can also use Transfusible Ink Markers for creating beautiful designs and text for the tote bag.

This project is made, keeping in mind the people who have just started or had to purchase their very first Cricut Machine. The instructions are kept simple, and only one layer is included to avoid confusion. Once you are used to making one-layer projects with ease, you can always make more complex and detailed designs. But to gain confidence, one must first master the most basic and straightforward projects.

Let us start making this beautiful and elegant tote bag. One crucial point to always remember whenever using transfer sheets, always mirror your design before cutting. If you cut the design without mirroring, the design will be cut inverted. In some cases, this might work out okay if you only have specific patterns and designs to cut. But in the case of text, you must mirror it. This point is repeated a lot of times in this book, because this mistake occurs very commonly.

(Beautiful Tote Bag)

- Cricut Maker Project Level: Easy (Beginner)
- Time: Start to Finish – 30 minutes

- Materials and Supplies:
  - Cricut Maker
  - Easy Press 2
  - Heat Mat
  - Canvas tote bag
  - Measuring tape
  - Butcher Paper
  - Heat Transfer Vinyl (Color of your choice)
  - Weeding tool
  - Standard grip mat
  - Cricut Fine tip blade
  - Scissors
- Instructions:

1. As in all projects, the first instruction is always to clear up your working space. It is really important to keep the working space clean and clear. This makes the steps of the project to be followed smoothly.
2. Collect all the materials and supplies required for this project.
3. Turn on your device or laptop and log in to Design Space.
4. Start a new project.
5. Click the text button. Write your favorite quote or your favorite saying.
6. Now edit the size and the font of the text.
7. Arrange and align it according to your design.
8. You can also use the rotate option to slightly curve your text.
9. Be creative.
10. The most important thing for this project is sizing.
11. You should always measure the size of your tote bag.
12. The design should not be tiny; neither should it be huge.
13. It should be of an appropriate size.
14. For a medium-sized tote bag, the design size should be 4 inches by five inches in length.
15. Align the design to the leftmost corner so that the rest of the vinyl van is saved for future usage.
16. Once you have aligned and sized your text, click the Make It button.
17. See the settings on the Prepare page are correct. Then move forward.
18. Now on the made screen, first select the heat transfer vinyl.
19. Next, mirror the image. This point is critical. If you forget this step, the design will be cut in the inverted orientation. In easy words, the design will be ruined.
20. When you are satisfied with everything else, set up your cutting Mat and attach the heat transfer vinyl to the Cutting Mat.

21. Let the Cricut Maker start its work, and you wait for the creative magic to happen.
22. Once the design is cut, remove the Sheet from the cutting Mat.
23. Cut out the design from the vinyl sheet and weed out the negative space.
24. Now heat the easy press 2 according to the instructions for a canvas bag.
25. Prepare the bag by rolling on the lint roller on it.
26. Put the vinyl on the tote bag. The vinyl should be placed in the center.
27. You can determine the center of the bag by folding it in half and ironing the centerline. This way, you will get the perfect center.
28. Place the vinyl in the center of the tote bag. Cover it with butcher paper.
29. Use the Easy Press 2 to press on the design for about two minutes and then remove it.
30. Take away the butcher paper and the backing of the transfer sheet.
31. Your beautiful tote bag is ready for use.

Conclusion

So, by now, you must have come to an understanding that the Cricut Maker is the holy grail for the creative soul. This die-cut machine offers you a plethora of possibilities. You imagine, and the Cricut Maker turns your ideas into reality. The best part about this device is precision and finesse. To attain perfection is the actual goal for a crafter, and this is precisely what the Cricut Maker offers.

The most outstanding feature of the Cricut Maker has is its ability to cut and shape more than 300 materials. It ranges from the softest, most fragile materials like crepe paper to much harder materials such as wood and leather. The other feature worth highlighting is that it is the only device in the Cricut Machines range with a rotary tool that cuts fabrics with precision and without any need for backing material. Now, this feature is greatly beneficial. You have an endless opportunity with fabric. You can make quilts, fabric dolls, accessories for little kids, and whatnot. You can use your creativity to make mixed medium projects involving fabrics. Perhaps an essential feature of this model is the Adaptive Tool System. This is extremely user friendly, and most importantly, any new tools that Cricut will launch will be compatible with the Cricut Maker. So, you will only be needing the Cricut Maker for all your future creative endeavors.

Another essential part of the Cricut Maker is the software. Design Space is the software to control and create on the machine. The best part about it is that the interface is quite simple and easy to use. Just a few clicks, and you can carry on with your creations and DIYs. You can download the Design Space application on your laptop or mobile and can even use it offline. In the Design Space, you can either create your project from the very beginning or choose from various projects already included in the program. Another feature, Cricut Access, is a subscription-based service that gives you access to hundreds of thousands of pre-saved projects to choose from.

So, if you are a creative person and love to create beautiful stuff for yourself, your family, friends, or even for business, then the Cricut Maker is just for you.

www.ingramcontent.com/pod-product-compliance
Ingram Content Group UK Ltd.
Pitfield, Milton Keynes, MK11 3LW, UK
UKHW051656191025
8470UKWH00027B/246